W9-AVW-011

GREAT BEAR FOUNDATION

FIELD GUIDE

to the

GRIZZLY BEAR

Lance Olsen

SASQUATCH BOOKS
Seattle, Washington

Printed in the United States of America

Cover design and illustration: Dugald Stermer
Text illustrations and maps: Robert Spannring
Composition: Scribe Typography

Library of Congress Cataloging in Publication Data

Olsen, Lance.
   Field guide to the grizzly bear : understanding and safely observing
Ursus arctos in western North America / by Lance Olsen.
      p.   cm.
   At head of title: Great Bear Foundation.
   Includes bibliographical references (p.).
   ISBN 0-912365-55-2 : $5.95
   1. Grizzly bear--North America.   I. Great Bear Foundation.
II. Title.
QL737.C27042   1992   92-8546
599.74'446--dc20   CIP

Published by Sasquatch Books
1931 Second Avenue
Seattle, Washington 98101
(206) 441-5555

Other titles in the Sasquatch Field Guide series:

The Audubon Society
Field Guide to the Bald Eagle

The Oceanic Society
Field Guide to the Gray Whale

American Cetacean Society
Field Guide to the Orca

International Society of Cryptozoology
Field Guide to the Sasquatch

Contents

Introduction

The grizzly bear is the ultimate symbol of true wilderness. It is a wide-ranging animal that requires vast landscapes. It survives best where the lands remain wild, roadless, and uninhabited by people. But grizzlies are reality as well as symbol. People are interested in knowing about that reality, and the bears in turn need our understanding.

Because a field guide to grizzlies can contribute to the mingling of two species that are potentially dangerous to each other, I've included advice in this book that is intended to reduce hazards to people and bears alike. These pieces of information should be regarded as tips, not guarantees. Anyone who ventures too near a grizzly bear must accept the burden of responsibility for that bear's welfare as well as his or her own. Sasquatch Books and the Great Bear Foundation urge visitors to grizzly country to learn more about safety than it is possible to go into in this book. An excellent source of detailed information on this subject is Dr. Stephen Herrero's book *Bear Attacks: Their Causes and Avoidance*, included in the bibliography on page 47.

Thanks go to the dozens of naturalists and biologists who have contributed to my understanding in ways too numerous to mention here. I'm especially grateful to Drs. John Craighead and Charles Jonkel for their years of patient sharing and teaching, and to Lorie Rustvold for inspiration.

Partial proceeds from the sales of this field guide help support the work of the Great Bear Foundation, which has established eight programs for the conservation of the world's wild bears. The grizzly is a top-priority species for the foundation and a cause célèbre for many other North American conservation groups whose actions contribute to the bear's survival on this continent.

Lance Olsen

Naming the Bear

To the Blackfeet Indian Nation of what is now Montana and Alberta, the grizzly was known as "the real bear." Some Blackfeet regarded the animal as so sacred and powerful that they would not—and even today will not—say its name out loud. A variety of names, including "grandfather" and "badger," came into use so that the grizzly could be discussed without making direct reference to it.

The famed explorers Lewis and Clark often called grizzlies "white bears," a reference to the sheen of the coats of individuals with white-tipped guard hairs. Mountain men and settlers later came to refer to the bear as "silvertip."

Modern scientists have classified and reclassified the grizzly bear. For many years the name *Ursus horribilis* was applied to differentiate the grizzly from the larger coastal brown bear, *Ursus arctos*. (The general view at that time was that brown bears live on the Pacific Coast and grizzlies live in the interior.) The two were regarded as separate species with separate geographical distributions.

It is characteristic of science to make such distinctions in its search for precision and technical accuracy. But in this case there were problems. For example, one observer noted that a brown bear could become a grizzly simply by walking up the coastal side of a mountain and crossing over into an interior valley. Today, scientists generally agree that the grizzly and the brown bear are members of the same bear species, *Ursus arctos*, that the European father of taxonomy, Carolus Linnaeus, identified in Europe two centuries ago. Subspecies are now recognized in North America; the exact number of subspecies worldwide is open to debate. Reports of fertile offspring from the union of polar bears and grizzlies have further muddied the distinctions that can be made among North America's bears.

Family Tree

Like the Europeans who would eventually endanger them, grizzly bears are immigrants to North America. Their ancestors—"brown bears"—had spread all across Asia and Europe by the time of the ice ages, when ice locked up enough of the earth's water supply to lower the level of the oceans, exposing much land and allowing the bears to reach this continent as well as Japan.

The Finnish paleontologist Björn Kurtén dates the origins of the world's bears to 20 million years ago, with the appearance of *Ursavus elemensis*, the "dawn bear." It might be possible to trace the evolution of bears even further back in history, to bear-dogs or dog-bears that were larger than the fox terrier–sized *Ursavus*, but it is in *Ursavus* that we first encounter the dental structure that distinguishes bears from dogs and other canids. Expanded chewing surfaces on the molars allowed it and its bear descendants to chew the grasses and other vegetation that are parts of today's bears' diets.

U. elemensis lived in subtropical forests during the Miocene epoch; its earliest fossils have been found in Germany. The range of this animal's descendants gradually stretched eastward into Asia, where the first brown bears—today's *Ursus arctos*—appeared during the Elster glaciation, about 500,000 years ago. About 250,000 years ago, the new bear's range expanded westward into Europe and northward into Siberia. From Siberia it reached North America, following the same path as many other immigrant species, including humans: land bridges exposed by the drop in the levels of the oceans.

Grizzlies have been geographically isolated from their Old World relatives since the end of the ice ages, roughly 10,000 years ago.

Modern Bears

Today, there are bears on every continent but Antarctica and Australia. In addition to the grizzly (*Ursus arctos*)—also known as the brown bear of Europe, Asia, and North America—seven species are currently recognized: the North American black bear (*Ursus americanus*) of the United States and Canada, polar bear (*Ursus maritimus*) of the Arctic, spectacled bear (*Tremarctos ornatus*) of South America, Asiatic black bear (*Selenarctos thibetanus*) of Central Asia, and the highly endangered sun bear (*Helarctos malayanus*) of Southeast Asia, giant panda (*Ailuropoda melanoleauca*) of China, and sloth bear (*Melursus ursinus*) of India. Biologists believe that within a decade or two, the current eight species could be reduced to five or fewer. The total number of the world's bears is estimated at one million, or about the same as the population of San Diego or Phoenix. Thus, according to estimates made in 1992 by *The Los Angeles Times*, more people are born every four days than there are bears in the world.

Facing page
Top: polar bear
Center: Asiatic black bear; sun bear; giant panda
Bottom: spectacled bear; sloth bear; North American black bear
Outside: grizzly bear

Distribution and Population Dynamics

Grizzly bears are now extinct in about 98 percent of their former range in the lower 48, some of their former range in Canada, and in localized areas in Alaska. As many as 50,000 to 100,000 grizzlies once lived in the lower 48; fewer than 1,000 survive there today, most of them found in the Rocky Mountains of Wyoming, Idaho, and Montana. A few may live in the Rockies of Colorado, and at least a few seem to survive in the North Cascades of northwest Washington. There are recent but unverified reports of one or more grizzlies in eastern Oregon's Hells Canyon. The few grizzlies of extreme northeastern Washington are bears whose home ranges straddle the Washington–Idaho–British Columbia border.

Once abundant in the province of Alberta, grizzlies are now almost entirely limited in that province to the Rocky Mountains along the western border. The bears are still found in more than half the neighboring province of British Columbia, although they are extinct on much of the southern lands adjacent to the state of Washington. Population levels in the Yukon and Northwest Territories probably remain near what they've been since the retreat of the ice sheets 10,000 years ago, and Alaska's 30,000 to 40,000 grizzlies make that state the foremost remaining stronghold of the continent's great bear.

Facing page
Approximate grizzly bear range

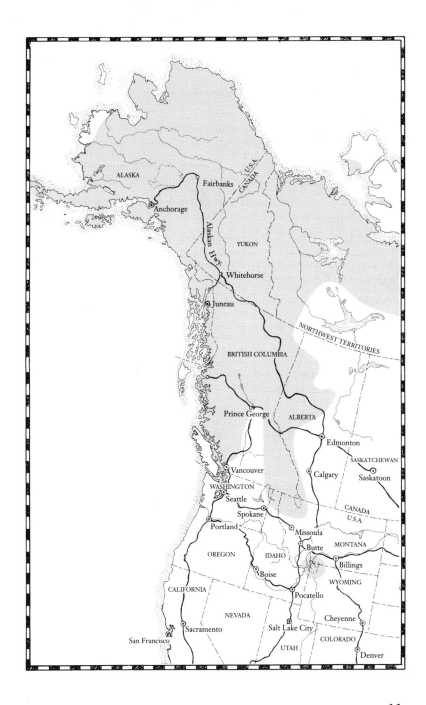

Population-Habitat Dynamics

Estimates of the number of grizzlies that constitutes a "minimum viable population" vary from less than 100 to more than 350. "Minimum viable population" has been defined as the number of bears needed to maintain a stable population for 100 or more years. World Wildlife Fund–Canada has estimated that a minimum viable population for grizzlies would be about 393 bears, but that a truly self-sustaining population that would not go extinct in about a century would have to be 10 times that number, or about 3,930 individuals.

These bears would need ample space. Just how ample is a question that demands further research, but millions of acres would certainly be required. This acreage would have to be productive enough to meet the needs of the bears. It would also have to provide the animals with freedom from human presence, active harassment, and killing. The key to the survival of a grizzly bear population is a four-part formula: one part population size (number of bears) plus three parts habitat (number of acres, productivity of the available acreage, and degree of security).

Although formally listed as threatened by the U.S. government, grizzlies continued to be targets for hunters in Montana until 1991, when the hunt was stopped through court action. Grizzlies are still hunted in Canada and Alaska.

Physical Characteristics

LIFE SPAN

Unknown. Age rings on teeth (called *cementum annuli*) can be read like rings on a tree. Some individuals have lived longer than 30 years in captivity, and one western Montana female lived more than 34 years in the wild.

Victims of poaching, habitat destruction, bear eradication programs, and to a lesser extent hunting, many grizzlies die at a fairly early age. Roads built into formerly undeveloped areas increase ease of access for poachers and hunters, shortening the life span of grizzly bears. Roads also increase disturbance caused by human presence and the likelihood that bears will suffer from aggressive harassment. Rural housing development, logging and mining operations, and resort and oil field developments break habitat down into fragments that are too small to support self-sustaining populations. Fragmentation of habitat decreases the lifespan of a population.

SIZE

Determined by gender and nutrition. Male grizzlies of coastal Alaska may reach weights in excess of 1,000 pounds (450 kg), females in excess of 600 pounds (270 kg). Male height can reach 9 feet (2.7 m); females are smaller. A male on Alaska's Kodiak Island may weigh 1,000–1,200 pounds (450–540 kg), and stand 9 feet tall (2.7 m), or 4 feet (1.2 m) at the shoulder when on all fours. Grizzly bears of the North American interior may reach weights in excess of 600 pounds (270 kg) for males and 300 pounds or more (120 kg) for females; standing heights of 8 feet (2.4 m) for males and 6 feet (1.8 m) for females.

SKULL AND TEETH

The grizzly's nose is higher at the end than between the eyes, giving a characteristic "dished-out" shape to the face—a helpful characteristic for identification in the field. Extremely powerful jaws, with 42 teeth.

CLAWS

Used most commonly for digging in soil for foods such as biscuit-root, front claws grow continuously and wear down with use. Grizzlies use their front claws, which are initially white or ivory colored, with considerable dexterity, moving them independently much as humans move their fingers to grasp and manipulate objects. They can also be used together as shovels for digging dens and digging for food. Front claw lengths of 4 or more inches (10.2 cm) are not uncommon. Hind claws are about 1 inch (2.5 cm).

COAT

Consists of woolly underfur and straighter, longer guard hairs. The guard hairs, which extend beyond the underfur and are the visible part of the coat, are often white- or gold-tipped. Variations in daylight can make for differences in the appearance of this silver-tipped hair, causing a single bear to be reported by two different people as two different bears. The hair, or pelage, is especially long at the shoulders. It is variable in color, from light blond to black. Layers of the heavy winter coat are rubbed in late spring and early summer, exposing the bear's lean condition at that time of year.

DIET

Omnivorous. Diet varies by season and includes grasses, roots, berries, nuts, insects, fish, and small and large mammals ranging from rodents to moose, elk, and mountain goats.

Field Identification

Grizzly range in North America overlaps that of the continent's other two bear species. One is the polar bear, readily distinguishable by its white or yellow-white coat; the other is the North American black bear. The similarity in the normal range of color for grizzlies and black bears, as well as the similarity in size of a small adult grizzly and a large adult black bear, creates potential for mistaken identity. Even experienced observers sometimes have difficulty distinguishing between the two, especially at a considerable distance.

In the field, the best means of identification is body shape, as illustrated on the facing page. Note the characteristically large hump (created by muscle mass) over the grizzly's shoulders, and the difference in the heights of the bears' humps and rumps. Also, the grizzly's dished-out profile contrasts with the black bear's, which is straighter, more "Roman-nosed." Experienced trackers use footprints to differentiate grizzlies from black bears.

Every year, mistaken identity causes hunters to shoot one species of bear that they've identified as another. In many such cases, officials rely on examination of skulls and teeth for positive identification.

Problems in identification can arise for novices and experts alike, because what is true for most bears is not always true for all bears. Some grizzlies resemble black bears more than other grizzlies do; a grizzly's characteristic hump may not be equally evident on every individual. The potential for mistaken identity is real, and, because black bears are generally more tolerant of humans than grizzlies, reducing it can increase your margin of safety.

Color is an unreliable guide for identification; like size, it can vary from bear to bear. Grizzlies range in color from light blond to black, but the possibilities are similar for the North American

Grizzly bear

Black bear

black bear. There are claims that grizzly bears can even be pure
white; Great Bear Foundation scientific adviser Charles Jonkel
has collected reports of these in western Montana, and white
grizzlies have also been reported in British Columbia. Apparently,
these are not albino bears, but simply a white-coated phase of
the species. The North American black bear has a white phase
too, in British Columbia, named Kermode's bear after the scien-
tist who first identified it.

Agility, Strength, and Play

Bears usually move about on all fours. They are quite agile and have been likened to acrobats because of their great dexterity; one grizzly was filmed doing a forward somersault as it ran along a mountainside. And grizzlies can run much faster than their usual lumbering gait suggests to the casual observer. While it is very difficult to obtain precise measurements of the running speeds of wild animals, experts have estimated that grizzlies can achieve speeds of up to 35 miles an hour (56 km/h) or faster for short bursts and can run several miles, although probably not at peak speeds.

Grizzlies can stand erect on their hind legs, but their ability to walk that way is very limited. A standing bear is most likely raising itself above tall grasses, brushes, or other obstructions to its view, or simply elevating its nose above ground level in search of a scent that will tell it something about its surroundings.

To agility and speed, add power. Grizzlies are extraordinarily powerful animals, capable of moving large boulders easily in search of prey — marmots, for instance — that may be hiding underneath. One researcher reported seeing an 800-pound (360 kg) male biting the neck of a 600-pound (270 kg) male and shaking it so hard that the smaller bear's feet left the ground and its body flew violently back and forth (the smaller bear survived). One large male in Montana brought down cattle by clamping its jaws on their backs until the pressure crushed and separated vertebrae.

It is worth noting that grizzlies make use of their great power selectively, only as needed. For instance, a bear that fishes for salmon but prefers to eat only the roe will press on the fish with one paw, just hard enough to squeeze out the eggs. Further, in most cases in which humans have been on the receiving end of a grizzly attack, the massive trauma that a grown bear can deliver was not inflicted. Most injuries are cuts and punctures (indicating some clawing and nipping) and sometimes broken bones; victims are not usually killed by the bear, even though the bear could easily do so. The most likely explanation is that the animals use their great power with restraint, carrying out most attacks on humans as warnings or reprisals and not with the intent to kill.

Grizzly cubs are good climbers, able to pull themselves up into trees. This mostly playful activity may occasionally prove essential to the cubs' survival—a way to escape predatory adult males, who rarely climb trees.

Grizzlies are excellent swimmers, easily navigating large, fast-flowing rivers and broad lakes. Their swimming is done not only out of necessity: they also swim for pleasure and enjoy playing in water. Photographer Doug Peacock videotaped an adult walking onto a frozen mountain pond, breaking through the ice, and then sitting down in the chilly water to play with a piece of the broken ice.

Since bears vary in temperament, playfulness can vary from one individual to the next. Adults have been observed "skiing" down snowbanks, some sliding down the bank and climbing back uphill to slide down again. Such skiing is often done on all fours, but at least one authority has seen tracks that suggested the grizzly had slid down a steep snowbank while standing on its hind feet.

An adolescent grizzly bear

Senses

EYESIGHT

There is a longstanding belief that bears' eyesight is not good. This may or may not be true. Naturalists have reported seeing grizzlies walk up to ridgetops to see the sunset, and others speak of bears avoiding fine tripwires set across trails to capture the bears on film. Clearly, it is possible that these conclusions were based on misinterpretation; a bear that happens to sit down with his face toward a sunset may not be seeing that sunset. Likewise, a bear that avoids a tripwire may have smelled it without seeing it.

Scientific controversy about the visual acuity of bears has arisen in part because of incidents in which bears did not seem to recognize humans as humans—a bear apparently would not see a person until he or she had made some movement that caught the animal's attention. Thus, some observers have concluded that while bears can see movement, their sight is not good enough to let them recognize the shape of an object that is standing still.

This and similar interpretations have been popular for many years, and have taken on an aura of fact. The bears' behavior lends some support to the belief: grizzlies are masters of what might be called "studied indifference," which means that they are capable of acting as though they do not see something that they are in fact fully aware of. Someone who sees a grizzly move by, grazing peaceably and never looking in the direction of a human observer, might conclude that the bear simply did not see him or her.

Yet at least some experts are adjusting their opinions about the grizzly's vision. Reports suggest that bears have color vision, and there is anecdotal evidence that European brown bears, close relatives of the grizzly's, can recognize their zookeepers as

individuals in a crowd of zoo visitors. Sharp eyesight unquestionably plays a key role in fishing for salmon and trout. Some Alaskan grizzlies will walk into salmon streams, put their faces into the water, and look for salmon swimming nearby, a technique called "snorkeling." Others learn to stand at places where salmon must negotiate waterfalls and catch the leaping fish in their teeth. Still others scan the shallows for the backs of salmon scurrying upstream.

SMELL

The Canadian naturalist Andy Russell quotes his father-in-law's quip that if a grizzly gets a whiff of you, it can tell you the color of your grandmother's wedding dress—an observation that pays fitting homage to the grizzly's highly developed sense of smell. A grizzly can detect scents whose sources are many miles away. Scientists have found evidence suggesting that black and grizzly bears can detect the odor of, for instance, beechnuts or elk carcasses at distances of 30 to 40 miles (48–64 km). More research is needed to explore this facet of bears' adaptation to their world, but all researchers agree that bears have an excellent sense of smell.

HEARING

Most experts are of the opinion that grizzlies' hearing may be similar to or better than that of humans.

RUBBING

Grizzlies enjoy scratching their backs against trees or similar objects such as telephone poles. This back-scratching behavior hints at some sensitivity of touch, whether to relieve an itch or to create a sort of self-induced "massage."

Grizzlies also touch each other, often gently. One reliable observer watching a mating pair of adults reported that the male sat quietly with his arm around the female. Mothers often hold and fondle their cubs, and the cubs touch each other and their mothers. This contact is probably not mere coincidence, and may express a genuine need in the health of wild bears. It is known from research on other species that a lack of such simple physical contact causes severe disruption in animals' relations with others of their own species.

COMMUNICATION

Grizzlies communicate with other bears and other species, such as humans, through body language, vocalizations, or a combination of both. A grizzly mother concerned about the security of her cubs may express the equivalent of, "Hey, I don't want a fight, but you're coming way too close and making me very nervous," by simply turning sideways to the approaching human. This is apparently an unlearned, instinctual behavior that bears understand and humans, unfortunately, often do not. A human who does not recognize a communication of warning from a grizzly can provoke an attack even when no provocation is intended. The bear's subtle communication (such as turning sideways and/or simply lowering the head) may go unnoticed by novice grizzly-watchers; bears who are patient or tolerant may then give further warning, such as a soft *whuff* or growl, or may simply move some distance away, an indication that they have been at least somewhat disturbed by the intruder. If the humans or other bears require further notice that they are in danger, the bear may move its jaw rapidly to click or "pop" its teeth, adding audible to visible warning. Other warnings are also possible, and most grizzlies will employ one or more of them in an attempt to avoid conflict. Newcomers to grizzly country are urged to study the book we list on bear attacks (see p. 47) for further information on this subject.

The Lives of Grizzlies

MATING

Grizzly bears mate in early summer. A male and female may stay together for courtship and mating that can last two weeks or more in areas where bears are thinly distributed. Where the population is—for bears—dense, males and females may mate with more than one partner per day. Males roam over larger home ranges than females do, in part to find females that will be receptive to mating. Males may have a home range of up to 1,500 square miles (2400 square km), encompassing the home ranges of several females, some of whom may be receptive to mating in a given year. Bears do not remain mated for life.

Females may begin having cubs at four years old in highly productive areas, but not until one or two years later in less productive landscapes. Grizzlies can reproduce for most of their lives; one female brown bear in a German zoo was still giving birth at age 26.

PREGNANCY AND GESTATION

Bears' gestation is unlike that of other mammals. When the sperm and egg of bears unite in a single cell, that cell divides until it reaches a stage of multicell development known as a blastocyst. In other mammalian species, the blastocyst implants itself in the female's uterine wall; in grizzlies and other bears, however, implantation is delayed. A grizzly that becomes pregnant in June will carry an unimplanted dormant blastocyst that will not further divide until the bear is in or ready to enter her winter den, which may be as late as October or November. It is at this point that the blastocyst will attach to her uterine wall and resume development. Cubs are born in January or February. This means that grizzlies have a short gestation period, about three months.

Not all pregnancies lead to gestation and birth. The critical factor is the condition of the female when she dens for the winter. A female that has not taken on enough reserves of body fat to meet her own and her cubs' needs may somehow shed the blastocyst before it attaches to the uterine wall. Factors that prevent females from taking on sufficient reserves of body fat include climatic influences on food supply and competition from other bears and/or humans for use of the landscape that provides bears with shelter and food.

THE CUBS

Cubs are born to the hibernating female in January or February and weigh approximately 1 pound (.45 kg) at birth. Litters range from one to four cubs, with two being the average. Again, the size of the litter depends on the female's condition. Initially, the tiny offspring are blind and helpless, covered with fine, short gray hair. Cubs survive on their mother's milk until late April or May. A female has six nipples and milk that is 25 percent to 33 percent fat—eight to ten times the fat content of human milk. On this rich liquid diet, the cubs grow rapidly; by late April or May they may have gained as much as 8 pounds (3.6 kg). Typically, mother and cubs will continue to draw down her fat reserve until the general growing season begins in June or July. By then, the cubs will weigh around 20 to 30 pounds (9–13.5 kg) each.

As is true for some other animals, such as rabbits, male grizzly bears sometimes kill and eat cubs, and scientists are studying that behavior to understand its evolutionary advantages. A male that kills a female's cubs may be killing the offspring of another male, in order to make the female receptive to mating with him and raising his own cubs.

GROWTH OF CUBS

Because grizzlies have such short gestation, and cubs are so small at birth, females must stay in the den until the cubs are grown enough to leave it. Even when leaving the den, some time in April or May, females cannot wander far from it. (In contrast, adult males—who den alone—can leave their dens earlier. Males do not help females raise the young.)

Cubs need time and play outside the den to gather strength for following their mothers across the sometimes rugged terrain of grizzly country. The family stays near the den for two weeks or more. When they venture away from the den, cubs begin to learn where to find food at different places and in different seasons. Cubs continue to nurse as they learn about other foods, and may nurse for up to two years.

This precise learning of food type, location, and season of availability is important to the cubs' eventual independent survival. Grizzlies have excellent memories and do not forget the locations of berry fields, root crops, or other foods that their mothers have lead them to. Once a bear learns the location of a food source, it will return to that place again and again.

By fall, the cubs will have grown to 50 to 110 pounds (22.5–49.5 kg). They now reenter the winter den with their mother. Cubs usually stay with their mothers for two years and may live with her for as many as four. Size of litter, rate of growth, and arrival of sexual maturity all depend on the landscape's productivity and the bears' freedom to move about in search of food. When the female is ready to mate again she will drive her cubs away; this usually happens during the cubs' second summer with their mother. The young females will usually share part of their mothers' home ranges, but young males usually disperse, which helps ensure against inbreeding. It may be because young males are not welcome near other grizzlies that they are displaced into areas frequented by people and consequently get into trouble more often than young females do. But all grizzlies establish at least part of their own home range by learning it from their mothers.

Hibernation

Some biologists have said that bears are not true hibernators. Others counter that in fact bears are more efficient hibernators than other species. The controversy arises because most hibernating species eat, defecate, and urinate at least sometimes during a winter of hibernation, but bears do none of these things during their five to seven months of winter sleep. The debate may actually boil down to the definition of hibernation, or whether there are different kinds of hibernation.

Hibernation length varies according to climate and food availability. In colder, northern climes where winters are lengthy, hibernation is also long. In these areas, foods are covered by snow in winter, and the growing season is short. Bears must therefore live by "summer wages"; they must gain enough of a fat reserve in as few as three months to ensure their survival through a lengthy winter and the following spring. In more moderate, southern climes, where winters are not long and severe and the growing season is longer, hibernation is accordingly shorter. Bears in captivity that continue to be fed do not hibernate at all, because they are assured of a year-round adequate food supply. In terms of energy, bears' lives are centered on a kind of "savings account" of fat.

Bears spend months of hibernation without taking in food or water, and without expelling wastes in urine and feces. For scientists, the question is how they do it. It is an important question. Although bears do not urinate during hibernation, their bodies do not accumulate the toxic urea that is ordinarily eliminated through urination. Understanding this process may prove invaluable for humans who suffer kidney failure and need costly dialysis to cleanse urea from their blood. Whereas in other species, including humans, such lengthy inactivity would cause the thinning and weakening of bones (a condition known as osteoporosis), scientists believe that during hibernation, bears recycle urea to make protein that builds bones.

Understanding urea recycling may also hold important clues for future human space travel, which may require human explorers to be dormant for many months. Other medical applications may come forth as more is learned about hibernation. For example, although bears live for months at a time on a reserve of fat, they don't accumulate cholesterol. Humans do accumulate cholesterol, which can result in heart disease. It seems the bears have a number of lessons to teach us.

THE GRIZZLY'S DEN

Grizzlies hibernate in dens. Den sites vary from region to region and from bear to bear. Regional differences determine the type of denning opportunities available. Individual differences may be related to individual learning experiences of the bears and/or the variation created in the ongoing evolution of the species.

Some grizzlies use natural caves for dens, where such caves are available. Some caves have been used for thousands of years. Where caves are scarce, most grizzlies dig their own dens, which are generally not reused, in part because some collapse after a winter's use.

Not all bears dig dens in the same way. Some dens are dug straight into mountainsides. Others begin as straight tunnels, then turn upward to sleeping chambers. A sleeping chamber elevated above the entry tunnel has the advantages of holding heat in the sleeping area and keeping the bear dry if melting

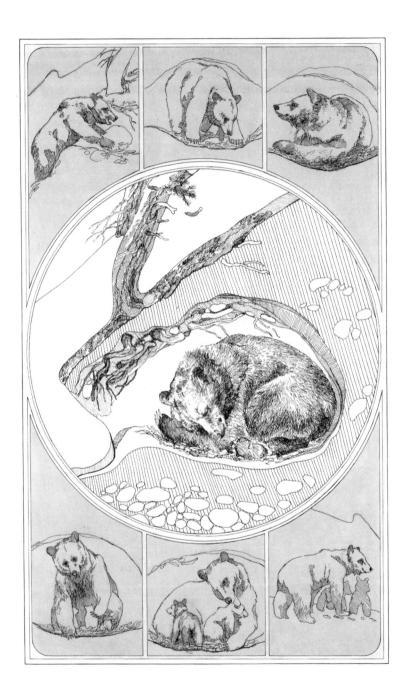

snow pours into the tunnel. It would be premature to either accept or reject the possibility that these effects are intentional. Females may possibly pass information about den construction on to their young by example.

Grizzlies prefer remote locations for their dens. Soils must be deep enough to allow digging, and the slope into which digging is done must be fairly steep, or the roof may be too thin to last all winter. Many bears dig dens under the base of trees, where roots help hold soil together and protect against collapse. The thick roots of grasses and other vegetation can also reinforce the roof and walls of a den. Grizzlies also show a preference for places whose topography and wind currents allow a blanket of snow to collect and remain all winter. This snow cover serves as insulation that traps heat in the bear's den. The combination of soils, vegetation, and other factors that makes a good site for den construction is not available everywhere and may be a limiting factor in a grizzly bear population in a particular locale.

Adult male grizzlies den alone. There have been reports of newly independent subadults sharing a den for a winter.

Foods

The great American naturalist John Muir once said that bears eat all but granite. This is especially so in areas where they must make fast weight gains during short summers in order to survive long winters. A female grizzly who will enter a winter den in late October and remain there until the following May must be prepared to sustain herself and one or more cubs on her food reserves. This means that she can hardly afford to pass up any food that is available to her. For example, she may rely partly on ants in midsummer, following a spring diet of fresh sedges and grasses and possibly the carcass of a moose or elk killed by winter storms and preserved in a snowdrift that will be melting when she and her cubs emerge from their den. Late summer and fall bring ripe berries. By fall, nutritious roots grown to full size after a summer's growth will also add to her fat reserves.

Some grizzlies learn to hunt, and will stalk and kill even the adults of large mammal species such as elk. Some will kill domestic cattle and sheep that humans place in their range. On the high slopes of the Rocky Mountains, grizzlies are known to subsist for periods on moths scooped from under rocks. Where trout or salmon fill streams, the bears learn to fish. But nuts, corms, tubers, and forbs are also important: in some areas, and especially at certain times of year, a grizzly's diet can be 80 percent vegetation. Although typically classified as a carnivore, or meat-eater, the grizzly is as omnivorous as the environment requires it to be for its own survival and the survival of its cubs.

Grizzly bears catch trout in Yellowstone National Park in Wyoming. Along the coast of British Columbia and Alaska, grizzlies have access to several species of salmon available in continuous runs throughout the summer and fall. As a result of this access to abundant food, the coastal bears tend to be bigger than those in the interior. In evolutionary terms, an animal with

33

the genetic potential to grow large can only do so when the environment supports that growth. A plentiful supply of fish is one such means of support. Rich environments thus allow for large bears, whereas environments that are not as generous select for smaller ones.

The productivity of the environment can also affect the bears' temperament. Some biologists believe that coastal bears are less aggressive than interior ones, perhaps in part because the abundance of food reduces competition. It may also be true that when a large number of bears gathers at one place—such as a falls on a salmon run—they are forced to develop a cooperative social order that may be less necessary where they are scattered across a landscape that can support relatively few of them.

Grizzlies learn their fishing methods from their mothers. The cubs of a female that waits patiently at one fishing spot for a salmon to leap near enough for her to catch in her jaws will learn that technique by observation and mimicry. When these cubs mature and the females have cubs of their own, they in turn will pass the tradition on to the next generation.

The kind of individual learning experiences that lead a bear to fish at a certain place using certain methods can also apply to hunting. For example, it may be that grizzly cubs whose mothers kill domestic sheep and cattle will follow in their mothers' footsteps when they are grown. It also seems that for grizzlies, as for humans, learning can be a lifelong process. There is evidence that adults learn by observing other adults. One adult male in Montana was not known to kill domestic livestock until after he had courted a female who did. This male seemed to learn from an adult other than his mother, although he preferred his own methods for killing livestock: while the female killed cattle by inflicting lethal wounds around the neck, the male did it by breaking the animals' backs and then biting their noses until they suffocated and died.

Bears and People

ADAPTING TO PEOPLE

Grizzlies are highly evolved, intelligent animals capable of changing their behavior as a consequence of learning. This includes learning to adapt to people. A bear that spends some of its time near humans and the rest in rugged, unpeopled terrain will behave differently in each area. For example, it may roam only at night when it is near humans, staying out of sight during daylight hours. When that same bear is in a remote area where people seldom venture, it will sleep at night and move about at sunup and sundown, or even in broad daylight.

This kind of adaptation, it should be noted, seems to be limited to the bears who have learned that humans can be dangerous. An unschooled young bear may show up in broad daylight in the backyard of a human residence, and bears who live in areas such as national parks, where they are protected from hunting, can be bolder and more aggressive in their approach to humans. These animals sometimes end up being killed for becoming a real or perceived threat to human safety. Some experts insist that eliminating hunting seasons results in unwary bears who are subject to new problems, and environmentalists debate whether it is really helpful to the bears to fail to let them know how very dangerous people can be. The topic becomes increasingly controversial as the human population continues its sprawl into bear country, pressing the bears beyond the limits of their ability to adapt.

KEEPING THE DANGERS IN PERSPECTIVE

The one thing people know about grizzly bears is that they can be dangerous. Unfortunately, this does not stop some people from acting carelessly, either deliberately or unknowingly inviting attack. It also does not stop others from *overestimating* how dangerous a grizzly can be.

How can people learn to keep the danger in perspective? Most human experiences with grizzlies are uneventful or even positive; people like to see grizzlies, and usually describe their sightings as wonderful, memorable experiences. But at least some element of risk remains, no matter how educated, experienced, and expert we may be.

It is important to remember that we are not discussing just one dangerous species when we talk about grizzly bears and people; we are actually talking about two. Proof of the danger that we create for grizzlies is easily seen in the fact that our species has driven theirs into extinction on a huge proportion of their former habitat. While grizzlies do sometimes pose dangers for us, we are far more of a threat to them.

One of the more stubborn myths about grizzlies is that their attacks on people are unprovoked. After all, it is common sense that no one would deliberately provoke a grizzly bear into an attack. But it's possible to provoke such an attack without intending it; most if not all attacks fall into this category. Others are not as easily explained, but still may be provoked by human action. For instance, there have been rare cases in which a grizzly bear has come out of the dark of night, into a human campsite, and killed and eaten a human being. This rare behavior may have something to do with the fact that almost all such attacks are made by grizzlies with a history of eating human food discarded in dumps or campgrounds. The situation raises challenging questions. Not all grizzlies that are exposed to discarded human foods will attack people; those that do are in the minority. It is far from clear why some bears that feed on food humans throw away are so-called killer grizzlies while most are not. It does seem possible that nature's most dangerous grizzlies are in a sense not nature's bears after all; instead they are made dangerous by human carelessness. They may have been "provoked" in ways we do not yet understand. That could mean that the victims were not the actual provokers of the attacks; the attacks by these bears may have been triggered unknowingly by people who discarded food where grizzly bears could get at it.

This is why park rangers and other wildlife officials are insistent that wild bears not be fed, and why they issue tickets and fines to people who break that rule. If you see anyone toss food to a grizzly bear, report the incident to authorities as soon as possible so that they can apprehend those persons before it happens again. Also report open dumps and unclean campgrounds, where grizzlies can acquire feeding habits that may lead some of them into serious trouble, indeed may lead to their being shot.

Safety Tips

The following section is an introduction to safety in bear country, it is *not* a complete list of safety measures. (Visitors can attain additional information from books such as Dr. Stephen Herrero's *Bear Attacks: Their Causes and Avoidance*.) Always check in at ranger headquarters or consult park officials for the most current information on grizzly conditions.

Keep a clean camp means that you should be scrupulous about food odors. Food odors include cooking odors. These odors may be carried on breezes to bears that are many miles away. A bear that smells them might be tempted to follow the scent to your camp. You can prevent this: after cooking and eating, wash all your utensils and your face and hands. The scent trail that could lead to your camp will be broken.

Don't let cooking odors get on your sleeping bag or tent. Move your gear out of the way of the campfire smoke and cooking area.

Unless you are very careful, you will probably get cooking odors on your clothes as you cook. If so, don't wear those clothes when you sleep, and don't keep them with you in your tent overnight. A grizzly's sense of smell is so good that even faint traces might be enough to tempt it to come investigate.

If you go on a hike that will keep you out on the trail for one or more nights, you will have no choice but to carry your food by day. But don't keep your food nearby at night. Experts recommend keeping food and backpacks 100 yards (90 m) or more away from a campsite. Hang your food and packs in a tree if possible. Bearproof containers are also advisable. Remember: Handling your food correctly can greatly increase your margin of safety, the safety of other people, and the safety of bears.

It's a good idea to keep the wind at your back when hiking in bear country. Traveling with the wind at your back puts your scent ahead of you, warning bears that you are coming, so they can move out of your way.

Pay attention. When in grizzly country, stay together, walk slowly, and make noise along trails. The less you hurry, the more time you will have for keeping watch for bears. This improves your chances of seeing a bear before you get too close. And don't rely on your eyes alone: listen, too. Bears can be very quiet, but they can also be noisy enough to let you hear them before you see them. A grizzly feeding on berries will probably be rustling the bushes. Listen for this. Don't rush. Go slowly. Give the bear and yourself plenty of time and opportunity to avoid conflict. Remember that pouring rain, a blanket of snow, or a howling wind can obliterate sounds you would otherwise hear. In the wilderness, expect the unexpected.

Keep your distance. Many people visit bear country in their cars and see grizzlies from the road. If the bear is 100 yards (90 m) or less from the road, stay in your car. If the bear is between 100 and 200 or 250 yards (180–225 m) from the road, it may be all right to leave your car, but do not leave the road. Because a grizzly can run at speeds of 30 miles an hour (48 km/h) or faster, the bear could reach you in a matter of a very few seconds, possibly before you were back in the safety of your car. Remember that young people move more quickly than, say, their grandparents, so plan accordingly. Finally, no matter how far from the road a grizzly may be, don't pursue it. Stay on the road. You may be able to sit comfortably by the edge of the road, set up your camera, and watch a bear that is 300 yards (270 m) or more from you, but it is bad manners and poor safety to leave the road and reduce the distance that the bear has decided to maintain between you. Take it easy. Give the bears and yourself a break. Respect the bear's chosen distance, and be ready to return to your car if a grizzly starts coming too close to you.

GRIZZLY ATTACKS

To err is human. No matter how hard we try or how much we know, we can forget or make a mistake. Or we may do everything correctly, but still get attacked by one of the rare grizzlies (or black bears) that kill and eat people. Other people, if careless in discarding human foods, may set us up for trouble with a grizzly.

The risk that a grizzly will attack humans with the intention to kill and eat them is very remote, and determining the intention of a bear is difficult. Should a bear's purpose to kill be unmistakable, however, experts say victims should NOT play dead. They should fight back with any and every means available: kick, hit, roar aggressively, and, if armed, shoot to kill.

If you are attacked by a female in defense of her cubs, on the other hand, authorities say that playing dead can be effective. If you fight back in this case, you will probably only make her attack you all the more vigorously, because you will confirm in her mind that you pose a real danger to her or her cubs. If you accept the attack submissively, showing her no sign that you want to fight, she will be reassured that it is safe to drop her attack, gather her cubs, and get away.

Actually, the term "playing dead" is not the most appropriate one in such cases, because the defensive mother bear probably has no intent to kill you anyway. She is most likely only scolding, punishing, and warning you for seeming to threaten her cubs. Let her see that you are not dangerous; do this by staying quiet and still until she leaves. Lie peacefully on the ground, and protect soft, vital areas of your body. To protect your throat, clasp your fingers across the back of your neck and pull your elbows together. To protect your stomach, pull your knees up to your chin and chest, and keep them there until you are sure the bear has gone. Some authorities say that an attack by a female with cubs is the kind of attack that people are mostly likely to survive, if they follow the tips given here.

If you encounter a bear near an animal it has killed, it is also best to act submissively by backing away. Do not play dead near the bear's kill, though — the bear wants you to be as far away as possible.

One final tip: a spray is now available that seems to have stopped charging bears from following through with actual attacks, as well as stopping attacks that were already in progress. It is called Counter Assault, and further information about it is available from the manufacturer, Bushwacker Backpack Supply, in Missoula, Montana. People who favor this spray also like it for being an extract of an organic material—cayenne pepper— that is not known to cause lasting damage to bears. Be warned, however, that having this spray is not an excuse to get dangerously close to bears, nor is it a substitute for common sense.

Where to Go to See Grizzly Bears

Experienced grizzly-watchers report that their best luck comes when they sit and wait. Grizzlies are mobile animals that move about extensively in search of foods. They may appear at any place at any time. A person on the move in search of grizzlies may arrive at places that bears have just left, or may encounter a bear at short range and provoke a defensive attack. Dusk and daybreak are good times to be watching for grizzlies. Any vantage point that allows a broad view of the landscape is especially good.

In a search for grizzlies, a good pair of binoculars can be far more useful than a strong pair of legs. To use binoculars effectively, fix the binoculars on one part of the landscape and search that field of view carefully before moving binoculars to adjacent terrain. Binoculars or a powerful-spotting scope can also bring a distant bear up close. This has two important advantages. The most obvious one is safety, for the bear as well as for the human observer. Seeing grizzlies at a distance of, say, 300 to 600 yards (270–540 m) or more also allows the observer to see grizzlies undisturbed, in their natural, wild condition.

Photography is a special challenge for people who visit grizzly country. In popular vacation posts such as Yellowstone National Park, cameras can be very dangerous if they are not used with caution and respect. The standard advice given to photographers is to "fill the frame with the subject." But wildlife photography at close range is usually a form of disturbance and harassment, and may trigger a charge or attack from a bear that takes offense at an impolite or threatening intrusion.

Suitable places for seeing grizzlies can change from season to season and year to year. Local regulations may also change as needed for protection of bears and people alike. Check with local environmental groups as well as agencies such as state or provincial fish and game departments. Ask where bears can be

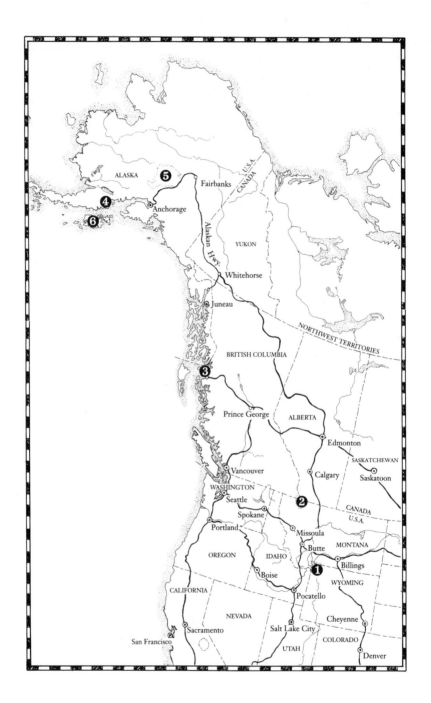

watched at considerable and considerate distances through binoculars or a spotting scope, or where there is careful supervision for viewing at shorter distances.

1. YELLOWSTONE NATIONAL PARK The oldest national park in the United States and its surroundings are home to an estimated 200 to 300 grizzlies. Every acre of the Greater Yellowstone ecosystem is important to grizzly bears; consequently, they may show up at any place, at any time. One site that offers a chance to see grizzlies at a distance that is healthy for bears and visitors is Hayden Valley, which offers roadside parking. Yellowstone officials and local groups such as the Alliance for the Wild Rockies and the Greater Yellowstone Coalition, both based in Montana, provide information on the ecosystem and its wildlife, including bears. You can request timely information about grizzlies at Park Headquarters or at any of the Ranger District offices located in the park. Conditions change from season to season and year to year, and advice changes accordingly.

Write: Yellowstone National Park
P.O. Box 168
Yellowstone, WY 82190
(307)344-7381
Recommended reading: *Track of the Grizzly* by Dr. Frank Craighead

2. WATERTON-GLACIER INTERNATIONAL PEACE PARK
In addition to Yellowstone, the vast majority of surviving grizzlies in the American West are found in and around Glacier National Park, which straddles the United States – Canada border and joins Waterton Lakes National Park in Alberta. The number of grizzly bears making use of land in and around Glacier National Park is estimated at 200.

As in Yellowstone, the bears' whereabouts vary with seasons and conditions.

Write: Glacier National Park
West Glacier, Montana 59936
(406)888-5441
Waterton Lakes National Park
Waterton Lakes, AB T0K 2M0
(403)859-2445

Recommended reading: *Grizzly Country* by Andy Russell

3. KHUTZEYMATEEN RIVER SANCTUARY The remote Khutzeymateen River flows into the Pacific Ocean on the coast of British Columbia north of Prince Rupert. Here, up to 50 grizzlies graze on lush estuary meadows, forage for salmon along the river, and move about in giant Sitka spruce—some of the last ancient forests remaining in the world. In June 1992, the BC government set aside the area as Canada's first grizzly bear sanctuary. The exhaustive campaign to see the area protected from the devastation of clearcut logging lasted over 20 years. Plans call for the area to be co-managed with the Tsimshian Indians, whose ancestors inhabited the Khutzeymateen for centuries. As part of a future management plan, guided bear tours may be allowed to continue in the sanctuary under strict guidelines.

Write: Valhalla Society
Box 224
New Denver, BC V0G 1S0
(604)358-2333

4. MCNEIL RIVER STATE WILDLIFE SANCTUARY The best-known opportunity to view bears at very close range is at McNeil River Falls in Alaska. This area is strictly supervised to ensure that the bears are not disturbed. Observers are admitted a few at a time, after obtaining a permit

through a lottery conducted by the Alaska Department of Fish and Game. On-site experts are available to answer questions about bear behavior, biology, cub-rearing, and other topics, including the rules of bear etiquette. Up to 60 bears have been seen fishing for salmon at McNeil River Falls at one time; some photographers have captured as many as 15 in the same photo. The sanctuary is accessible by seaplane and a short hike. Visitors bring their own sleeping bags and can stay indoors overnight in a modest shelter. Bears move freely about the entire area.

Write: Alaska Department of Fish and Game
333 Raspberry Road
Anchorage, AK 99518
(907)344-0541

5. DENALI NATIONAL PARK AND PRESERVE Alaska's Denali National Park offers spectacular vistas across a broad landscape that is home to an estimated 200 to 300 grizzlies. Hiking and overnight camping are allowed with permits issued by park officials. Park officials can also provide the required bearproof containers for food carried in backpacks. Buses traveling on park roads help reduce pressure on wildlife from traffic and provide opportunities to see bears.

Write: Denali National Park and Preserve
P.O. Box 9
Denali Park, AK 99755
(907)683-2294

Recommended reading: *The Grizzlies of Mt. McKinley* by Adolph Murie
Grizzly Cub by Rick McIntyre

6. KODIAK NATIONAL WILDLIFE REFUGE The Kodiak Island National Wildlife Refuge was set aside as a bear refuge by President Franklin Roosevelt in 1941. This island off the south central coast of Alaska's mainland has

been a wilderness paradise for some of the largest bears on Earth. Perhaps as many as 10 percent of all the grizzly bears in Alaska live on Kodiak, although these bears may be of a different subspecies of brown bear than those usually regarded as grizzlies. The animals are spread widely across the island and are often seen at streamside during salmon runs. Permits are required, and a limited number are available. The U.S. Fish and Wildlife Service maintains cabins for rent in the refuge.

Write: Kodiak National Wildlife Refuge
1390 Buskin River Road
Kodiak, AK 99615
(907)487-2600

Recommended reading: *Monarch of Deadman Bay* by Roger Caras

For Further Information

BOOKS

Numerous good books have been written about the grizzly bear. Book-length discussion of the animal provides richness of detail that can't be matched in other formats. Each of the following books provides important information for people who plan to visit grizzly country.

Caras, Roger, *Monarch of Deadman Bay* (Boston and Toronto: Little, Brown, & Co., 1969)
A work of inspired fiction that follows the life of one bear from birth to death on Alaska's Kodiak Island. Realistic insights into a bear's relationships with humans and with other bears.

Carey, Alan, *In the Path of the Grizzly* (Flagstaff, AZ: Northland Publishing, 1986)
This book informs through its many photos of grizzly habitat as well as its text.

Herrero, Steven, *Bear Attacks: Their Causes and Avoidance* (Piscataway, NJ: Winchester Press; New York: Nick Lyons Books, 1985)
Detailed description of actual case histories of bear attacks on humans, analysis of why the attacks occurred, and information on how they could have been avoided. No better compilation of safety tips is available. This book also helps bears by showing humans how to reduce conflict with them.

Hoshino, Michio, *Grizzly* (San Francisco: Chronicle Books, 1986)
Informative photos of the bear's habitat, family life, agility and power, eating habits, and other behavior.

Russell, Andy, *Grizzly Country* (New York: Knopf, 1967)
The book is a classic, describing the bear's plight as accurately as any more recent book does. The author grew up and raised his own family in grizzly country.

RESOURCES

Alliance for the Wild Rockies
P.O. Box 8731
Missoula, MT 59807
(406)721-5420

> *Bozeman Office:*
> 127 W. Main, Suite F
> Bozeman, MT 59715
> (406)586-0180

Great Bear Foundation
P.O. Box 2699
Missoula, MT 59806
(406)721-3009

Greater Yellowstone Coalition
P.O. Box 1874
Bozeman, MT 59771
(406)586-1593

Speak up for Wildlife Foundation
Box 506, Station G
Calgary, AB T3A 2G4
(403)246-9328